A souvenir guide

Godolphin
Cornwall

Michael Sagar-Fenton

National Trust

Origins of Godolphin

Records of a dwelling at Godolphin go back at least 800 years, though its origins are probably far older. Peaceful now, its past carries stories of enormous mineral wealth, heavy industry, agriculture, high political office, war, decline, ruin and eventual rescue – a living timeline through Cornwall's history.

Godolphin estate is located in a sheltered valley, protected from the winds of West Cornwall by the hill. As well as offering protection, Godolphin Hill provided much of the estate's wealth.

The estate's standing structures, the house and its outbuildings, do not present a unified whole, but instead offer something far more intriguing – a visual portrayal of the many dramatic chapters of Cornish history through which the estate has passed.

Right Godolphin Hill provided both protection and wealth to the family that claimed it

A brief history

Cornwall's extraordinary variety of minerals brought it to the attention of the wider world long before the resourceful and mercantile Romans arrived in the first century AD. Godolphin's estates were rich in both tin and copper, and its earliest mines are believed to date from the Bronze Age (2500–800 BC). (For more on Cornwall's mining history, see pages 10–11.)

The present house is at least the third we know of built on the site. The first surviving reference, from 1166, identifies a house belonging to an Edward de Wotholca. Then, from the report of a robbery in 1307, we know there was a house here in which a family with the name of Godwalgham lived. It was possibly this transgression that prompted Alexander de Godolghan (d.1349) to build a small castle or fortified house around 1310, complete with garden, both to protect and display his wealth.

The site has been subject to continuous change, as the fortunes of the people who lived here waxed and waned. The Godolphin family (as they came to be known) prospered, rose to political eminence in Tudor England, recovered their position after the disastrous Civil War of the 1640s, only for their line to die out, causing the estate to pass to the Dukes of Leeds in 1785.

The buildings fell into disrepair and, following the decline of the tin industry, the estate functioned simply as a tenanted farm. In the 20th century the property passed through the hands of various owners, but in 1937 it was sold to Sydney Schofield, marking another change in its fortunes. The Schofield family did much to maintain and improve it before the estate was sold to the National Trust in 1999. Some years later, in 2007, the house, gardens and farm buildings were also bought by the National Trust. At this time the process of rediscovering and restoring Godolphin's multi-faceted past began in earnest, and, as you will see, it is still going on.

Farly occupation

The earliest records of Godolphin, dating from 1166, refer to a family variously known as Wotholgha, Gotholgan and Godolghan, thought to have arrived with the Norman Conquest 100 years earlier. They were not the first occupants of the site – there are signs of habitation from the Bronze Age – but they made it their home and its natural resources made them very wealthy.

Sir Alexander de Godolghan, estate landlord and local collector of tithes, needed a house that reflected his status, and so in around 1310 he built his 'castle' a little way to the south-east of the current house. This was not so much a castle as a fortified house with a large courtyard, set in the centre of what is thought to be one of Britain's earliest recorded formal gardens. From here the family established themselves through wealth from the estate's mines as well as farming and rents. Additionally, later that century, a judicious marriage did much to boost the status of the Godolghans in Cornish society.

Combined fortunes

A Godolghan daughter, Eleanor (born c.1376), married neighbouring landowner John Rinsey, combining two estates. They obtained permission to build a chapel in each. This was the only place of worship built on site in Godolphin's history, as generations of the family attended nearby Breage church, where many of them are buried. The members of the combined family originally styled themselves

Left Worked masonry is found all over the site and used in both practical and decorative ways

Right A Godolphin helmet hanging in Breage church

after the names of both estates, but soon dropped the Rinsey title. However, despite the combined wealth from two estates, by the mid-15th century the dwelling at Godolphin was described as being 'in ruins' by English chronicler and antiquary, William of Worcester (1415–82).

A grand design

Nothing remains of the 'castle' because in 1475 John Godolphin (John I) demolished the old house, established a new site and set about building a house he thought would more properly reflect his wealth and status. Indeed, it was to become one of the most celebrated and important Cornish houses of its time.

Pieces of granite were carried the short distance from the demolished building to the new site a little to the north-west, but many were discarded on the way. One of the fascinating features of Godolphin is the extraordinary quantity of dressed granite that you will see lying at shallow depths all over the estate. This may be in the form of paving stones, window mullions, arch-pieces, gutters and other worked pieces whose purpose must be guessed at.

The ghost of a great house

John I's new house, built in 1475, of which several illustrations survive, had grand architectural ambitions and was intended to far exceed and surpass what had gone before. As well as using masonry from the demolished house, the construction of the new house destroyed the careful symmetry of Sir Alexander's garden, being set at a different angle.

The siting of John I's 1475 house even required the diversion of the road from Marazion to Penryn from the side of the house to its current position about 180 metres further north. Its original aspect was towards the west, the direction from which visitors now arrive. This is hard to imagine, as the spectacular north frontage now dominates the scene, and the Stables have obscured the west side entrance, where a gatehouse once stood. The north face was originally just a curtain wall with two towers and a central gate.

Medieval remains

Inside the entrance was the first courtyard, as it still is. Two ranges of two-storey buildings face each other across the courtyard. The east wing (on the left as you enter) dates from this period, a splendid medieval survivor, and gives the best impression of the design of the whole of the living quarters, though the roof would originally have been thatched. These were the family apartments. Opposite were grander apartments for distinguished visitors, along with the Great Chamber, now the King's Room. By 1600 a privy garden had been walled in adjacent to the Great Chamber, the delightful King's Garden we still enjoy.

The great kitchen, chapel, stores and undercroft occupied the ground floors. However these were all incidental to the main feature, what is now the 'ghost' of the great house, the Great Hall.

The Great Hall

This huge, battlemented two-storey building was situated directly opposite the current entrance gateway, providing a suitably magnificent dining hall for entertainment and dancing, with numerous small apartments for guests and an inner courtyard. A contemporary account boasted that the house had 100 rooms and 40 chimneys and, though that was certainly an exaggeration, one may imagine it was one of the most important and imposing buildings of its period west of Exeter. Now only the porch entrance and some of the walls and window openings of the Great Hall (now reduced to a single storey) remain to remind us of its magnificent heyday.

Opposite The remains of the Great Hall viewed from the south

Below The view through the current entrance to the original porch entrance

A well-connected family

By the time the house was built in 1475, the Godolphins were Cornish landowners and people of rank. Under the Tudor monarchs (1485–1603) they prospered as never before, and John I was made High Sheriff of Cornwall in 1504. Their wealth came mainly from the tin trade, enhanced by the now extensive farming estates.

The family inter-married with many of the other great families of Tudor Cornwall – the Arundells of Trerice, the St Aubyns of Clowance and St Michael's Mount, the Boscawens of Tregothnan, the Carews of Antony, the Grenvilles of Stowe, the Killigrews of Arwennack and many others (see over).

John I's son, William I, was also created High Sheriff of Cornwall and the King's Warden of the Stanneries (tin mines) of Cornwall and Devon. Son of William I, also William, distinguished himself in battle under Henry VIII, in particular during the siege of Boulogne in 1544, when his contingent of Cornish miners succeeded in tunnelling under the castle walls (see page 34).

Protector and pioneer

The dashing Sir Francis I, nephew of William II, was the complete Elizabethan gentleman and soldier. He was Deputy-Lieutenant of Cornwall during the wars with Spain, responsible for the protection of the whole western coastline. As Governor of the Isles of Scilly he built the exquisite Star Castle, which still dominates St Mary's, the largest of the islands. However, his finest hour came in 1595 when, with a small group of local militia, he held back Spanish forces, which had landed in Mount's Bay and burned Penzance, Newlyn, Mousehole and Paul. Sir Francis sent word to another Sir Francis, the famous Sir Francis Drake, for reinforcements; meanwhile his heroic stand protected his county from greater losses.

At home at Godolphin, Sir Francis I poured his energy into improving the efficiency of his mines. This still depended on manual labour for extraction, but Sir Francis I brought over two German engineers who made great improvements to the crushing of the ore and the smelting process. A regular visitor to Godolphin was Richard Carew of Antony. It was from Sir Francis I that Carew obtained the extensive mining knowledge contained in his seminal 1602 work *The Survey of Cornwall*.

Top The Godolphins married into various Cornish families, including the St Aubyns of St Michael's Mount

Above Star Castle on the Isles of Scilly, built by Sir Francis Godolphin for the defence of the South West coast

A living by the seashore

In addition to what could be mined and harvested from their holdings, the Godolphins profited from another potentially lucrative, albeit less reliable source. Mount's Bay had a notorious reputation for shipwreck among sailing ships. As owners of a long stretch of the foreshore, the Godolphins were entitled to the bounty of any wreck salvage – provided they could secure it before local 'wreckers' had picked it clean.

Loyal subjects

Francis I's heir was another William, who married Tomasine Sidney, an heiress from Norfolk, in 1604. Like much of Cornwall the Godolphins were Royalists, and remained so as the divisions widened which ended in the Civil War. Sidney, middle son of William III and Tomasine, was one of the founders of the Cornish army in defence of the King, and was a poet, MP and prominent leader until he was killed in a skirmish outside an inn in Chagford, Devon in 1643.

Two years later, at the Battle of Naseby in Northamptonshire, the main army of King Charles I was destroyed by Oliver Cromwell's New Model Army. Taking flight to gather support for the king in the West of England, Prince Charles reputedly stayed at Godolphin overnight (in a room that, despite the lack of any documentary evidence, was ever after known as the King's Room) before escaping to the Isles of Scilly, where he was protected by Sidney's elder brother, another Francis who owned Godolphin and was Governor of Scilly. However, the Godolphins' fortunes were to pay the penalty of their steadfast loyalty to the Crown.

Lucrative links

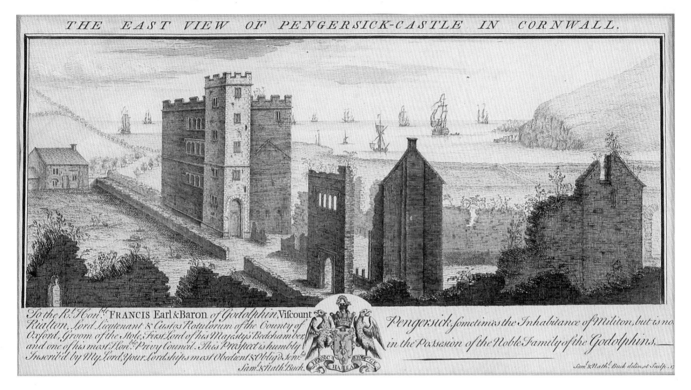

THE EAST VIEW OF PENGERSICK-CASTLE IN CORNWALL.

To the R.t Hon.ble FRANCIS Earl & Baron of Godolphin, Viscount Rialton, Lord Lieutenant & Custos Rotulorum of the County of Oxford, Groom of the Stole, First Lord of his Majesty's Bedchamber, and one of his most Hon.ble Privy Council. This Prospect is humbly Inscrib'd by My Lord, Your Lordships most Obedient & Oblig'd Serv.ts Sam.l & Nath.l Buck.

Pengersick, sometimes the Inhabitance of Militon, but is now in the Possesion of the Noble Family of the Godolphins.

Sam.l & Nath.l Buck delin.et Sculp. 17

Although Godolphin was the premier residence in West Cornwall, it had close associations with two neighbouring estates. The upper levels of society in the far West comprised very few families, all very familiar with each other, leading Carew to comment that 'all Cornishmen are cousins'.

One was Pengersick Castle, owned by the Pengersick family, prominent in Helston from the 14th century. In around 1400 they were granted permission to establish a chapel at the same time as the Godolphins' similar wish was granted.

By 1500 the property was owned by the Milliton family. John Milliton was favoured by the Tudor king Henry VII, who looked to his castle as part of the sea defences against the French. However, he is better known today as a sinister presence, one among the many ghosts said to haunt Pengersick Castle.

The other neighbour was the famous castle of St Michael's Mount. This had been a monastery since the 6th century and had accumulated various lands and endowments, which provided a steady source of income. Originally part of the establishment of Mont St Michel in France, it was owned by Syon Abbey until the Dissolution in 1539 when Henry VIII disbanded all Catholic institutions. It was then leased by the Crown to the aforementioned John Milliton of Pengersick, or perhaps to his son William. William had married a Godolphin, Honor, in 1535.

Above The East View of Pengersick Castle in Cornwall, inscribed 'Pengersick, sometimes the inhabitance of Militon, but is now in the possesion of the Noble Family of the Godolphins'

A South West View of St Michael's Mount in the County of CORNWALL, a Seat of Sir John St Aubyn Bart

The mystery of the *Santo Antonio*

Such is the tangled connection between these local families, and the Godolphins were also linked to the St Aubyns of Clowance, near Crowan. These connections came to a head when a treasure-ship belonging to King John III of Portugal, the *Santo Antonio*, was wrecked at Gunwalloe Cove in January 1527, carrying a cargo of solid silver and copper ingots valued at over £18,000. As soon as the storm subsided, local wrecking gangs came out in force, but it seems the three local landowners managed to secure the main bulk of the treasure.

King John sued Henry VIII for the return of his treasure, an embarrassment at a time when Henry was looking to annul his marriage to King John's cousin, Catherine of Aragon. Henry convened the medieval Court of the Star Chamber and word was sent to John St Aubyn, local Justice of the Peace, to conduct an enquiry into the treasure's whereabouts. St Aubyn duly convened a panel in Helston consisting of himself, Milliton and Godolphin, which reported after a decent interval that the matter remained, alas, a mystery. By coincidence the properties at Clowance, Pengersick and Godolphin all enjoyed substantial improvements in the following years, including the complete reconstruction of Godolphin's west wing.

The St Aubyn family eventually acquired St Michael's Mount, which they bequeathed to the National Trust in 1954.

Tin mining in Cornwall

Tin mining in Cornwall began around 2000 BC and is currently dormant following the closure of South Crofty Mine, Camborne in 1998. Four thousand years of mining inevitably had a huge impact on both the natural landscape and social history of the county.

Illustrations Plates from *De re metallica* ('On the Nature of Metals'), a book cataloguing the state of the art of mining, refining and smelting metals, published in 1556 and the authoritative text on mining for the next two centuries

'No greater tynne works in all Cornwall than be on Sir William Godolphin's ground....'

John Leland (*c.*1503–52), English poet and antiquary

The development of iron tools around 800 BC enabled the early miners to expand their activities enormously. They could clear forested ground more easily, gather firewood for smelting and, with the hard metal tools, attack the ground with purpose. When Greek geographer Pytheas of Massalia travelled to Britain in about 325 BC, he found a flourishing tin trade.

However, the miners still did not have the tools or technology to follow a deposit deep into the granite ground. Instead, they hacked away as best they could. Even by the time of Richard Carew's 1602 *The Survey of Cornwall* things had changed little: 'To part the rocks they have axes and wedges with which mostly they make speedy way, and yet not seldom a good workman shall hardly be able to hew three feet in the space of so many weeks.' The greatest advance came at the end of the 17th century with the use of explosives, in which the Elizabethan Francis Godolphin was an early pioneer, though this of course carried its own hazards.

As miners delved deeper underground, their conditions became increasingly harsh. Timber for shoring up the roofs was always in short supply in Cornwall, and the enormous quantity of underground water was a constant hazard. Along with the risks of rising water and foul air, the exhausting business of ascending and descending slippery ladders and crawling bent-double claimed many miners' lives; and that was before even beginning the strenuous business of extraction. Few miners lived to see their fortieth birthdays, and their pay bore no relation to the labour involved. However, on the other side of the coin, the rewards for successful mine-owners like the Godolphins were colossal.

Using the Land

Although Godolphin's principal business until the late 19th century lay beneath the ground rather than upon it, the estate was not given over solely to mining but supported a variety of uses.

Great houses like Godolphin commanded large estates supporting multiple tenanted farms, but they also had their own 'home farm' together with grounds and gardens designed to make the household as self-sufficient as possible. When there was more produce than needed, it would be taken to market at Helston, Marazion and Penzance.

The medieval palate, or at least the palate of the better off, had no taste for vegetables, which were regarded as the food of the poor. For the Godolphin table only meat and fish would do. Deer parks were not only a source of venison but also a proof of status, and Godolphin's deer park was created in the 16th century when the family was at its most wealthy and influential. The deer were contained by a high stone 'pale', sections of which are at least 400 years old and still visible today. From the top of Godolphin Hill, extending all the way down to the garden, the park was prominently sited so as to impress.

Also still visible and intentionally so, are Godolphin's 'pillow mounds' – man-made oblong mounds with flat tops built for raising rabbits for meat and fur. These pillow mounds are the finest examples to be found in Cornwall, two of them built on the skyline so they could be easily pointed out to visitors from the house.

The menu was completed by fish either from the estate's own 'stew ponds' (see page 20) or bought in from the local fishing ports of Mount's Bay or St Ives.

Keeping things sweet

Although the garden provided little in terms of vegetables, it was important for the growing of herbs and spices, for flavouring but mostly for medicinal purposes.

Fruit was always popular, and Godolphin's orchards warrant a book of their own (but are briefly described on pages 18–19). These were enhanced by beds and bushes of native soft fruit, such as strawberries, raspberries and gooseberries.

Finally, the keeping of bees was vital in ensuring the sweetness of puddings and 'bee boles' are still in evidence at Godolphin – the alcoves in the south-facing wall of the King's Garden in which straw 'skeps' would have housed colonies of bees.

Left A view of farmland from the top of Godolphin Hill

Right A skep in a bee bole in the King's Garden

The lie of the land

The long history of the Godolphin estate is written all over it: the scars of its industrial past can be seen along with the remains of the buildings that powered it; and when its fields and woods were pressed into agricultural production, they were given names that are still in use and give clues to the people who lived and worked here.

Much of the estate's activities were made possible by the River Hayle. Cornwall's mining history was always bedevilled by the lack of coal and timber, which had to be imported at great cost, so waterpower was at a premium. Many of the waterwheels that powered flourmills, tin-crushing mills, mine pumps and farm machinery were placed far from the river. The technique was to cut a watercourse known as a 'leat' from the river and lead the water to the desired spot, where it could power the waterwheel. Several natural underground streams flowed into the estate from the surrounding hills, including two running through the home farm.

Above Heather has colonised the estate's former mining areas and spoil heaps

Above The upper slopes of Godolphin Hill were enclosed to form a deer park, the stone boundaries of which are still visible

Clues in the names

The pattern of fields tended to radiate from the top of Godolphin Hill and extended as far as the river. The field names tell many stories, from the merely geographic such as the Mill Fields, the Big Downs and the Groves; others carry personal names such as Wilson's Downs and Mary's Downs; some mention outlying farms like Carsluick and Gwedna; and others speak of past uses, such as the Warren on Godolphin Hill, which yielded a rich harvest of rabbits, and a field still known as Deer Park. Nearer to the house are found Upper and Lower Horsepark and Fatten Close.

The 'Downs' fields higher on Godolphin Hill were enclosed in 1878 on the order of the Duke of Leeds as an unemployment relief programme to support the impoverished miners. Hedges on the estate were either of the dry-stone variety, filled with small rocks called hearting, or of the Cornish variety, which are stone-faced banks of earth. Since Godolphin Hill was popular hunting country, each new 'hedge' was built with a hole to allow hounds to pass through.

Godolphin, from the Cornish: *go*, 'little'; *dol*, 'valley'; *phin* or *fince*, 'of springs'

A cottage industry

The making of cider in Britain increased after the Norman Invasion of 1066. Apple cider was widespread in Northern France and, as Britain proved unsuitable for growing grapes for wine, it increased in popularity as an alternative to ale.

Western counties proved most successful for cider apples, because of the mild climate and plentiful rain, although Cornwall was less favoured because of the high winds, except in sheltered valleys like the Tamar. Most farms grew a few cider-apple trees for their own use, and from the 18th century it became customary to pay part of farm-labourers' wages in cider, sometimes up to a fifth of their due, until this was finally stamped out in 1887.

Sweet pickings

Godolphin was clearly highly favourable for apple growing and a substantial orchard was established to the north-east of the house. This served far more than the estate's needs and grew into one of the many small industries within the farm complex. The current Cider House (see pages 44–45) was built in the 18th century. The casks were probably made on site and the cider was sold widely. An account of 1727 from just one company shows sales worth £26 16s 8d in a single year, a significant contribution to the estate's income.

Many Cornish varieties of cider apple were grown, with local names such as Tommy Knight, Lord of the Isles, Captain John Broad and the Rattler (now the name of a popular draught cider). There is even a Godolphin apple, described in *A Treatise on the Culture and Management of Fruit-trees* (1803) by William Forsyth as 'a very handsome large fine fruit, streaked with red on the side next the sun'.

Godolphin's orchard was replanted in the early 1800s by a tenant farmer called Richard Tyacke, but by 1840 it had been almost entirely removed and an auction sale in that year included a significant number of disused cider casks. That sale coincided with the tenancy of John Rosewarne, who was a staunch Methodist. The committedly tee-total Methodism of tenant farmers almost certainly contributed to the demise of cider-making at Godolphin.

Nature's bounty
As well as their agricultural worth, cider-apple trees played a great part in ceremonies. In Cornwall on the nearest Saturday to Hallowe'en, varieties of large apples appeared in the shops, known as Allan Apples (probably from the Cornish *kalan gwav*, the first day of winter). These were eaten for luck, and girls sometimes put them under their pillows to dream of their sweethearts. In some western towns Allantide rivalled Christmas for the exchanging of gifts. As in most of the West Country the ceremony of Wassailing took place, most often on Twelfth Night. The farm workers would select a particular tree to salute by splashing it with cider, sing wassail songs accompanied by a fiddle, fire a gun to ward off evil spirits, and of course imbibe a great deal of the product.

Opposite **The restored Cider House and the old orchard**

Other enterprising uses

As a great and wealthy estate, Godolphin was the natural hub of the area, employing large numbers of people with a wide variety of skills. In addition to its orchard, Godolphin had a number of sidelines to supplement its income.

One valuable by-product of the orchard was slow-growing apple wood. This was exceptionally hard – as those who had to saw and shape it by hand would have agreed – and it often replaced metal as a component of machinery, in particular the cogwheels in mills and pumping engines. Its usefulness was not only due to its toughness, but also its ability to lubricate itself, saving a great deal of maintenance.

Fresh fish everyday

The 'stew ponds' were a feature of the gardens from early in their development, probably dating from the 16th century, although the smaller pond may have existed prior to the 1475 house. The ponds were refreshed by one of the underground streams and were used not only to cultivate fish for the house, but also to cleanse and preserve fish caught in other ponds and rivers, especially in the polluted mining ponds. They were effectively a reservoir of fish, of great value when refrigeration was unknown, ideal for domestic use or for sale. Poaching in the stew ponds was a very serious offence. In the 19th century the ponds became dry. It is believed this was due to the tenant farmers diverting the stream in order to use it over a water wheel at the end of the barn. Unfortunately there was insufficient water to make it effective and it was abandoned, but the water never returned to the ponds.

Above An aerial view of the garden, showing the outline of the stew ponds once stocked with fish

Right Leats cut from the River Hayle were found to be a source of ochre

Windward windfalls

Wrecking has already been mentioned. The landowners were entitled to the salvage from wrecks, but local people were always alert and fell on a wreck in huge numbers, sometimes emptying the mines of men. When a member of the Killigrew family attempted to put a lighthouse on Lizard Point, local people objected furiously, saying that 'he took God's grace from them'. The 'maritime trap' of adverse winds between The Lizard and Land's End, combined with bad navigation, made an end to literally hundreds of vessels. It was a sporadic if heartless source of income, the greatest bounty coming from the *Santo Antonio* in 1527 (see page 11).

Manifold minerals

A later and unexpected enterprise was the exploitation of ochre. The estate's mineral wealth included tin, copper, lead, zinc, tungsten and arsenic, and also small quantities of iron. The residue of silt in the pools and leats was considered a nuisance needing clearance, but in the 1890s tenant farmer Rosevear Rosewarne realised that the quantity of ochre – iron oxide – in the silt was a valuable resource. It was in demand for house paints, artists' pigments, preservatives and, combined with oil, for the protection of fishing-boat sails (hence their traditional reddish colour). To exploit this opportunity two new settling ponds were established along with a tramway and a drying house, and the enterprise prospered for several years.

The Rise and Fall of Godolphin

Between the 15th and 18th centuries, the Godolphin family rose to its highest prominence in the affairs of Great Britain and the house achieved its greatest architectural pretensions, before falling by slow degrees into neglect, obscurity and near ruin.

The face of Godolphin

By the early years of the 17th century the Marazion–Penryn road had been diverted and a more convenient and imposing entrance to the house and grounds added, the private drive of which still exists. However this brought visitors face to face with the plain north wall of the house, which was not considered sufficiently pleasing.

Francis, the older brother of Sidney the poet and soldier, took on the challenge in 1627. The splendid double colonnade of massive Tuscan columns was created and the hugely impressive covered gallery – the 'face' of Godolphin forever more. The original gateway and the carved double doors were preserved, and are still in place. To complete this part of Francis' ambitious project, the upper floor was constructed to form a spectacular link between the east and west wings.

The western gatehouse and entrance had already been abandoned and the beautifully proportioned stable block was erected in its place in around 1595. It remains virtually unchanged, although its proximity, attached to the main house rather than situated at a discreet distance, remains something of a puzzle, leading some to think it may have been a count house for the tin mines rather than a stable.

Loyalty rewarded

These works were intended to be just the first phase of the remodelling of the whole building, garden and grounds in a similarly formal style. However, in 1642 the country descended into Civil War. The Godolphins stood firmly for the King, even sacrificing one of their sons in his cause – the aforementioned Sidney.

During Cromwell's Commonwealth, most of the Godolphin lands were seized and Sidney's younger brother William was briefly imprisoned in Fleet Prison. Older brother Francis, who is said to have taken in the fugitive Prince Charles, paid dearly for his loyalty and he was disbarred from sitting in Parliament in 1644 and his estates confiscated. The Godolphins managed to retain the house and sufficient land to sustain themselves, but they were constantly watched.

When the Restoration came, Charles II did not forget his loyal Cornish supporters. Another Sidney was born, to Francis after his marriage to Dorothy Berkeley, and was appointed a Page of Honour at Charles' court, rising spectacularly through the ranks to become Lord High Treasurer. He was created Earl of Godolphin in 1706, a title that passed to his son, another Francis.

Opposite **The north front of Godolphin House**

Above **Francis Godolphin (1605–1667) remodelled the house and gave us the imposing entrance front we see today; by Cornelius Johnson**

Schooling the Godolphin way
The Godolphins gave their name and family motto – *Franc ha leal eto ge*, Old Cornish for 'Frank and loyal thou art' – to two schools. Charles, son of Francis III, married his cousin, Elizabeth Godolphin of Coulston in Wiltshire, and in 1726 they founded Godolphin School in Salisbury for the education of eight young orphaned gentlewomen. A prospectus of 1789 promised a regime of early rising, 'agreeable exercise' and a diet of wholesome books 'such as enlarge the heart to Virtue and excellency of Sentiment'. In 1861 the Godolphins founded a boarding school for boys at Hammersmith, West London. However, in 1905 it was re-established as a day school for girls, associated with the Latymer Foundation and taking the name of the Godolphin and Latymer School.

The Earls of Godolphin

The expansion and increasing magnificence of the house peaked before the Civil War. After the Restoration it remained a great house, but the ambitions its owners had for it diminished as they became increasingly involved in London life.

Sidney, 1st Earl of Godolphin, as Queen Anne's Lord High Treasurer, was as well-connected in Court and Parliament as he was remote from Godolphin. Of particular significance was his relationship with John Churchill, 1st Duke of Marlborough. Marlborough's leadership of the armed forces during the War of the Spanish Succession in the early 1700s saw Britain rise from a minor to a major power. However, for all Marlborough's skills as a military commander, this would not have been possible without Sidney, Lord High Treasurer, who effectively financed these campaigns. Among his many achievements, he was involved in the founding of the Bank of England and he was instrumental in negotiating and passing the Acts of Union 1707 with Scotland, which created the Kingdom of Great Britain.

Top Sidney Godolphin, 1st Earl of Godolphin

Right Henrietta Godolphin (née Churchill), 2nd Duchess of Marlborough; by Francis Kyte, after Sir Godfrey Kneller

The end of the line

Francis was married to Henrietta, Duchess of Marlborough, daughter of the Duke of Marlborough, who acquired a scandalous reputation as the mistress of the playwright William Congreve. It was generally believed that Congreve was the father of Henrietta's youngest child, Mary, to whom Francis gave the family name of Godolphin.

The couple already had another daughter and a son, William, a dissolute youth who died in 1731 at the age of 31 before inheriting his title. A younger branch of the Godolphin family had settled in Trewarveneth in Newlyn, but the Godolphin name had died out there by 1689.

Other branches had settled in Shropshire and Wiltshire, but on the death of Francis Godolphin, cousin of Francis, 2nd Earl, in 1785, there was no direct male heir left.

Mary had married Thomas Osborne, 4th Duke of Leeds in 1740 and so with her death and the male line of her family name having come to an end, the estate finally passed out of Godolphin hands to her widower.
It was hoped that the Dukes of Leeds would take an active interest in their new country seat, however the 4th Duke never came to Godolphin. In fact although their ownership of Godolphin spanned 135 years, they only visited twice. The main bedroom on the north-east corner was expensively remodelled with an arched window in honour of the visit by the 5th Duke of Leeds in 1790. On that occasion bonfires were lit on the hills to welcome him and his wife, but for all the fanfare, the Duke stayed for just nine days and returned to his ancestral home, Hornby Castle in Wensleydale, never to return.

Right **Francis, 2nd Earl of Godolphin**

The Godolphin Arabian

Sir Francis, 2nd Earl Godolphin, is responsible for making the family name world famous and enshrining the Godolphins in equestrian history, when he bought the horse that became known as the Godolphin Arabian. This stallion came originally from Yemen and was bought and sold several times before coming into Godolphin ownership, but Sir Francis recognised his potential and set him up in a stud in Cambridgeshire. His very first offspring won the Queens Plate at Newmarket nine times, and his other foals were so fast and successful that the Godolphin Arab became the highest-prized sire in England, and is credited with being one of the three ancestors of all today's Thoroughbreds.

Tales from Godolphin

The Godolphins were prominent at the highest levels during some of the most turbulent and exciting periods of English history, and their life-stories read like the pages of a dozen historic novels.

William Godolphin was a noted soldier in the service of Henry VIII, and when the French port of Boulogne proved resistant to a long siege in 1544, William led a company of Cornish miners overseas. Their task was to tunnel under the walls and plant mines, which they did with great success, even though none of the miners could be understood by anyone but William, as they only spoke Cornish. William paid the personal price of half his nose for his bravery, and the antiquary Richard Carew noted: 'He demeaned himself very valiantly beyond seas, as appeared by the scars he brought home, no less to the beautifying of his fame, than the disfiguring of his face'. He was knighted, given the honorary title of Governor of Boulogne and presented with the cast-iron royal coat of arms still on view in Godolphin.

Left The royal coat of arms presented to William after the Siege of Boulogne in 1544

SIDNEY GODOLPHIN.

From a Drawing in the Possession of the Earl of Orford.

& from a Painting then in the Hands of the Earl of Godolphin L.d High Treasurer of England.

husband's family in Breage church, though she was concerned that 'the expense should not be very great'. Her grief-stricken husband disregarded cost and had her carried to Cornwall on a hearse drawn by six horses in black, in a journey that lasted a fortnight. At the end of each day her coffin was taken indoors to be surrounded by lighted tapers and watched all night. Margaret had her final wish and was finally interred in the family vault at Breage, where a small brass plaque can still be seen.

Sidney Godolphin, the poet, was a learned and cultured man, who attended Exeter College, Oxford, and later represented Helston as MP in 1628–29 and again in 1640. Despite being famously tiny in stature, he took up soldiering for the king as a trooper in the cavalry army of Sir Ralph Hopton when the Civil War broke out in 1642. He was shot dead in a skirmish outside an inn in Chagford in Devon, and was buried at Okehampton church.

One of the most poignant tales is that of Margaret, wife of Sidney, 1st Earl of Godolphin. She was a noted beauty and scholar and a protégée of the diarist John Evelyn. She married Sidney in 1675. Three years later she gave birth to a son, Francis, but sadly died of a fever a few days later. Margaret had never visited Sidney's ancestral home, but she left instructions in her will that if possible her body should be taken to Cornwall so that she could lie with her

Engraved by W. Humphreys.

Mrs Godolphin

From an Original Painting in the Collection at Wootton.

Godolphin runs to ruin

The transfer of Godolphin to the Leeds estates saw it relegated from a cherished country home, however little visited, to just another piece of property and source of income. Consequently the mine-workings became of infinitely more significance than the neglected and almost incidental house and farm.

Although the high-flying Godolphins of the 18th century had spent little time at their Cornish seat, it was maintained to a decent standard. However, with an absentee lord, the quality and pretensions of the house rapidly declined. Few visitors spent time here. The tenant farmers confined themselves to the east wing and the rest of the house was given over to the accommodation of their servants and farm staff. The Great Hall was already in a poor state and grew ever more dilapidated and dangerous, until it was finally demolished in 1805, along with the southern part of the east wing where the library, chapel and many parlours had stood. The deer park fell into disrepair and the last deer was killed in around 1830. The gardens became overgrown or were turned over to growing vegetables, and the orchard had ceased production by 1840.

Below Ruins of mining works on the Godolphin estate with Tregonning Hill in the background

Exhausting resources

The tin mines, meanwhile, prospered. The introduction of explosives in the late 17th century transformed the pace of mining, achieving in seconds what would formerly have taken weeks, though with the attendant hazards of the somewhat unpredictable explosions. Thousands of tons of tin and copper poured out of Cornish mines, making their fortunate owners and shareholders exceedingly wealthy. The countryside in the richer tin-fields became industrial wastelands, full of waste tips, smoking chimneys, sheds, pumping engines and the thunder of the stamping machines that broke up the ore.

Godolphin in name only

The Godolphin name did not completely disappear with the end of the male line. Mary and Thomas Osborne, 4th Duke of Leeds, had three sons and a daughter, all of whom had Godolphin as a forename. Their son Francis Godolphin Osborne (above) was briefly MP for Helston, as was his second son, yet another Francis. When this Francis was elevated to the peerage, he styled himself 1st Baron Godolphin of Farnham Royal in Buckinghamshire. George Godolphin Osborne, 10th Duke of Leeds (below), sold the estate in 1920, thereby ending their connection with Godolphin. On the death of the 11th Duke in 1963, the titles passed to the 12th Duke, his cousin D'Arcy, who died without an heir a year later, finally bringing to an end the noble title of Duke of Leeds.

Back to the land

Above Godolphin's 19th-century farm buildings are gradually being restored

While the 17th and the 18th centuries were the heyday of the Godolphin mines, by the 19th century the once great house had become simply the farmhouse for the estate, admittedly somewhat grander than most, but fallen far from the ambitions of the Godolphins.

Following the passing of Godolphin to the Dukes of Leeds in 1785, the property was leased to a number of tenant farmers. Farming went through more mixed fortunes than mining, but the Napoleonic Wars (1793–1815) made many farmers and landowners very wealthy, who prospered due to the lack of competition from imports. However, this was not enough to prevent Godolphin's fine medieval farm buildings from declining as the Dukes of Leeds, being absentee landlords, did not maintain them. The estate's purpose in previous centuries was to sustain the family and its household, but the 19th-century farm was now a commercial enterprise. When the medieval buildings were pulled down, the tenants built good-quality farm buildings using the redundant granite, most of which are still standing.

Practical and productive

Cornwall's principal crop has always been grass, nurtured by its warm winters and plentiful rainfall. The most significant harvest of the year was hay, always fraught with the threat of rain during the long period of hand-mowing, turning, drying, gathering and packing into hay-ricks. Horses were replacing oxen as draught animals, but cattle were the mainstay of most Cornish farms. Milk was sold locally in a raw state, but mostly processed into butter, cheese and cream for market. Calves were also sent to market, walked all the way to Helston, Marazion or Penzance, and pigs, hens, geese and ducks joined the list of cash crops.

The large two-storey barn cut into the hillside was designed so that hay and grain could be carried into the upper storey on the level and let down via hatches to the stalls or calves' houses below. Pigs were often left to wander the farmyard, and shut in the Piggery only at night. Cows were kept indoors during the winter, each chained to an individual stall under cover.

Rising up the hill to the south of the main house, the two ranges of facing shippons are as valuable a historic relic as any of Godolphin's buildings. They were built on the typical pattern with a long feed passage, a stall (once of cobbles and later concrete) with a wide drain, and room for the farm workers to milk and to clean. At Godolphin the farm buildings are unusually close to the house, indicating a loss of pretension and delicacy regarding the scents and sounds of animal husbandry. At the top of the shippon range is the bull-pen. Bulls were generally not allowed out (hence their fierce reputation if they did break free) but securely confined except when needed. It's easy to imagine their frustrated bellowing echoing around these ancient buildings.

Below left The Stables and Piggery

Below right The back of the Piggery, now a tea-room

A romantic ruin rescued

The property reached its lowest ebb in 1920, when it was sold by the 10th Duke of Leeds to the sitting tenant, Peter Quintrell Treloar. By then it was in a very poor state, the ancient buildings of the west wing being used to store potatoes, and pigs housed on its ground floor. It was sold twice more before a family of an artistic persuasion decided they must have it.

Sydney Schofield was the second son of Walter Elmer Schofield, known as Elmer, an American Impressionist painter of the Pennsylvania school. Elmer visited St Ives at the turn of the 20th century to paint, adding the Cornish coast, harbours and cottages to his repertoire of grand Pennsylvania snow scenes.

While in St Ives, Elmer met Herbert Lanyon, a composer, pianist and photographer. Sydney

Left Godolphin photographed in the early 1900s

Above Walter Elmer Schofield, painted by his son Sydney in around 1940

Above Godolphin's stew ponds in the snow, by Walter Elmer Schofield

Right Sydney and Mary Schofield at Godolphin

sometimes painted in Cornwall with his father and first encountered Godolphin when it was recommended to them as a good subject to paint by Herbert's wife, Lilian.

This encounter with Godolphin left a lasting impression on Sydney, who had trained at the Slade School of Art in the early 1920s, but eventually decided to pursue a career in farming. On hearing that Godolphin was up for sale in 1937, Sydney bought it and moved to farm there, and in 1940 married the Lanyons' daughter, Mary. In 1938, his parents moved in and Sydney briefly took up painting again, his best work from this period being the series of portraits of St Ives fishermen on display at Godolphin. After the Second Wor ld War, Sydney rarely painted, since the rescue and repair of Godolphin House became his principal passion.

The start of the restoration

With some local help the Schofields devoted themselves to the long process of restoring the house to something of its former glory. Sydney was a member of the Society for the Protection of Ancient Buildings (SPAB), which influenced the philosophy of their approach to conservation; principles which the National Trust continues to observe today (see page 45). When Sydney died in 1983, Mary continued to live in the house. Their son John carried on the work to restore the house and gardens. He was helped by his Canadian wife, Joanne, and the couple took up residence in the granary.

Theirs was not an easy task. The fabric of the house had developed many serious structural problems. Most urgent of these was the state of the main timbers over the entrance, which had rotted to a dangerous degree. With the help of a large English Heritage grant in 2003 this was partly remedied, but this sadly proved to be only one of several major threats to the building. Despite the Schofields' heroic efforts in fund-raising and involving local people in their conservation work, it was simply becoming too much.

The National Trust bought the main part of the 600-acre estate in 1999 with a view to opening it up to the public with safe pathways through the mining areas. The risk remained that the house and gardens might be sold piecemeal for development, and so the Trust bought the whole property in 2007. Mary Schofield died the following year, having seen the house into safe hands.

The Latest Layer

The purchase of Godolphin by the National Trust was the end of one chapter but very much the beginning of another. It began a process of steady and painstaking restoration and conservation work, designed to uncover every phase of the estate's development over its long history.

Left The Great Hall façade is lightly planted with climbers to suggest elegant ruin rather than dereliction

Right The east wing from the rose border in the side garden

Current custodians

The first task of the National Trust was never in question. It was quite simply to stop parts of the house from collapsing. Despite the Schofields' earlier work, which surely saved the house from ruin, the restoration of the house required root and branch work on a large scale.

The timbers of the north front had been ravaged by centuries of wet rot, woodworm and deathwatch beetle. Many had to be replaced with new oak beams, and the structure was pinned together with around 300 metal braces and 5½ tons of steel. The entire roof of the north front was taken off so that its timbers could be repaired or renewed, and before the original slates were re-fixed, fire walls were installed and new entrances fashioned for the resident population of bats.

The spacious 1630 saloon in the north front was re-established by removing some Victorian partitions and, like much of the house, it was re-plastered, insulated and painted with distemper-type paints. New utilities were installed along with new bathrooms. Restoration was also carried out in the east wing, where the Schofields had lived, including the modernisation of the medieval kitchen. The total cost of the work on the house amounted to almost one million pounds.

At the same time, work was being carried out on the Piggery, now a tea-room, the former granary building and other parts of the complex. The long, careful task of sympathetically developing the gardens began, and the Cider House was conserved and reopened in 2015.

The remains of today

Visitors are welcome to explore all public areas at their leisure, but the guided tours which take place at regular advertised intervals are highly recommended for a fuller experience. Here, briefly, are Godolphin's architectural highlights.

Visitors to Godolphin arrive from the car park in the woods to the west of the house. The first building on the right is the former Piggery, a single-storey building which, since restoration, functions as reception, shop and tea-room (with a wonderful selection of cakes). Some of the giant pieces of slate which once divided the pig stalls remain as part of the structure.

Next on the right are the 400-year-old Stables, currently housing a collection of farm wagons. The mullioned windows, cobbled floors and gullies are all original and of fine quality.

A gateway on the line of the medieval roadway leads through to the main house forecourt and a circular lawn. An alternative route to the house through the gates from the historic drive affords a wonderful reveal of the north façade as you approach. Sydney Schofield replaced a monkey puzzle tree that once stood on the lawn with a folly made from two items relocated from elsewhere: a piscina standing on an apple crusher. The piscina, a bowl used for washing communion vessels, may be from the long-since demolished chapel that was used by the Godolphins in the 14th century. The apple crusher, as you might expect, came from the Cider House.

A door into the past

Arriving at the front colonnade, the original wooden doors open into the courtyard. On the left as you enter is the entrance to the hallway and house reception area. The range of buildings on the left is the oldest in the complex, dating back to the 1475 dwelling, although the roof would once have been thatched. On your right is the remodelled west wing, the visitors' accommodation including the King's Room, with an undercroft and storeroom beneath.

Opposite the entrance gate is the inner wall and gate of what was once the Great Hall, the ghost of the medieval house, best viewed now from the south.

An outdoor tour

Continuing past the front colonnade leads you through to the gardens. On the north-east corner of the house is the arched, stained-glass window of the main bedroom, said to have been redesigned for the visit of the 5th Duke of Leeds.

A path leads up past the small gardens on the east side, and passes the quirky 'potting shed', understood to have been built by John Schofield. The lane between the Stables and the Piggery leads into the sublime King's Garden, a square walled enclosure, beautifully arranged with lawns, box hedges and flowerbeds.

Leaving the King's Garden, retrace your steps along the lane and on your left you pass a detached two-storey building, formerly a granary and smithy. Behind the main house, climbing up the hill, are the two facing ranges of shippons or cowsheds.

The other main building in this area is the large L-shaped granite barn, behind the Piggery, built into the side of the hill, with an adjacent modern Dutch barn.

Opposite top The original doors dating from the 16th century

Opposite bottom The arched window of the main bedroom, remodelled when Godolphin passed to the Dukes of Leeds

Above The King's Garden and entrance to the King's Room

An ancient survivor

Godolphin's garden is a wonder of its own, one of the earliest fully realised designed gardens in Britain, dating from a time when most important houses were surrounded either by defensive walls and ditches or by open parkland. Around its paths and lawns would have walked the cream of Cornish society and their well-connected guests.

Indications are that the original 1310 house stood in the centre of a grid of nine square garden enclosures to the south-east of the

current house, some of whose borders can still be discerned. The removal of the building to its present site at a different angle destroyed this symmetry, but the grandeur of the new 1475 house was more than matched by the extraordinary beauty of the new garden.

It was laid out in the formal Italianate style fashionable at the time, with ornate flower beds and geometric paths, fountains and ponds, gilded statues, bowers and grassy walks; an exotic jewel in the middle of the untamed Cornish countryside.

Top The sunken lawn in the side garden

Above Detail of the 1791 survey plan showing the house and Great Garden at Godolphin

A walk in ancient walls

The enclosed King's Garden, as well as being an ideal environment for the growing of tender herbs, was an intimate outdoor space for those in the house. A particular feature of the gardens are the wall walks around the side garden – elevated paths along grass terraces on wide rubble walls. To the east and south these have now become dominated by trees.

Sycamores are a significant feature of the wall walks. Although many have fallen victim to old age or gales, many of the stumps have sprouted anew, perhaps coppiced for a while and then grown once more into mature trees. The north wall walk is still unobstructed and gives the perspective the designers intended, that the gardens should be viewed from above as well as wandered through.

Attached to the eastern part of the garden was the orchard, and to the north it is likely there was a water garden. South of the main garden walls is a long straight avenue, now tree-lined, once used for driving deer towards the hunters' guns and later as a horse or dog racecourse.

Below The rubble wall of one of the garden's elevated walks

Hidden treasures

Godolphin, like most ancient houses, has many quirks and corners, as you might expect of a house and estate with 600 years of building and destruction, growth and decline. Here are just a few curiosities to look out for as you explore.

The covered entrance beneath the mighty colonnade was not just an impressive frontage, but also provided an outdoor all-weather play-space for generations of Godolphin children. One of their games was skittles, in which a wooden club was thrown rather than rolled, and several shallow depressions can be seen carved out of the floor's granite slabs where the skittles once stood. More prosaically, as a contemporary photograph shows, the colonnade was later used as a covered car park.

Inside the courtyard, looking up to the left where the east wing joins the front, one can see that they do not in fact meet. This is because the spectacular 17th-century north front was intended to be connected to the east wing once that had been completely demolished and rebuilt in a similar style. Due to the Civil War this never happened, and so the buildings remain partly detached.

Left Godolphin glimpsed from the side garden

Left The covered
colonnade was once a
rainy-day venue for skittles

Left below Francis
Godolphin's architectural
plans were interrupted by
the Civil War as seen by this
break between the north
front and east wing

At the rear of the barn is a large Victorian wheel pit where a waterwheel would once have stood, probably intended to power mining work and eventually used for slicing up turnips for cattle feed. It is believed that there was insufficient water to turn the wheel, so it was abandoned. There was another, smaller waterwheel on the side of the Piggery. Slabs covering the pit can still be seen.

The south-facing wall of the King's Garden has a fine array of bee boles, small compartments where bees were kept in round straw 'skeps' (pictured on page 15). One or two skeps would be preserved through the winter, however the only way to extract the honey was to kill the bees by burning sulphur, and thankfully skeps gave way to more sustainable wooden hives.

There are several rewarding walks around the Godolphin estate. One leads to the well-preserved Leeds Shaft engine house, another passes the former Count House (mine offices) and Blowing House (where the tin would be extracted by smelting), and another leads around both banks of the River Hayle adjacent to the main Godolphin mine workings. The most popular walk passes up through the 'Slips' to the summit of Godolphin Hill, with its breathtaking views over the landscape and Mount's Bay. Beneath the ground are miles of deserted and flooded galleries from the mining past, and approximately 150 mineshafts have been catalogued, not all of which have been 'capped' or fenced off, so it's very important to stick to the paths. These are just a few of the varied walks to be enjoyed across the wider Godolphin estate.

Doing things differently

The National Trust's ambition for Godolphin is a mixture of ongoing and large-scale conservation work and the desire to provide an enjoyable experience for visitors. These people experience something quite unlike visits to other National Trust properties and, such are the plans for Godolphin, a repeat visit may be a quite different one.

Continuing the restoration where the Schofields left off was just one of the responsibilities of the National Trust when it acquired Godolphin. Now and for the foreseeable future, the Trust must attend to the other tasks of conservation and restoration around the property. In this it benefits from the immense support of scores of volunteers, who carry out many essential roles: welcoming visitors, giving guided tours, organising walks and special events in the gardens, as well as physical work around the gardens and estate.

Below With so much yet to be unearthed, Godolphin is a protected archaeological site requiring a sensitive approach to gardening

Holidaying at Godolphin

The house is available for much of the year as a high-quality holiday let. Visitors have access to Godolphin's gardens and estate all year round, and there are still opportunities to see inside the house at particular times.

Very briefly, inside the east wing is a stone-flagged entrance hall, a superb dining room with a carved oak ceiling and excellent Tudor linenfold panelling, and a modern kitchen.

Upstairs there are three bedrooms in the east wing and a small cosy sitting room. Above the colonnade there is a large drawing room or saloon with two further bedrooms in the west wing.

Among its internal treasures are a Venetian chandelier, plaster friezes and a fireplace surrounded by Delft tiles. The King's Room is usually open to the public, as are the ground-floor storeroom and undercroft beneath it.

Gradual growth

When the National Trust turned its attention to the gardens, it was decided that they should not revert to a formal reconstruction of any particular period, but should evolve in a sympathetic way from what was already here.

As a protected site, digging in the garden is restricted to a single spade-depth, and for the most part the gardening team works without the use of chemicals, with perennial weeds painstakingly pulled by hand.

Above **The main bedroom with Venetian chandelier and Georgian stained-glass window**

Left **Carving on an overmantle dated to the early 1600s, once part of the Great Hall but now in the King's Room**

Careful conservation

While Godolphin's orchard is unlikely ever to return to its former fruitful glory, the Cider House stands as testament to the time-honoured West Country tradition of cider-making. Recently restored, it will stand for many more years to come.

The 18th-century Cider House stands in the eastern meadow, probably on the foundations of an even older structure adapted from a mine building. During the heyday of the orchard, this building was the heart of the commercial cider-making process. The apples were picked and stored on the upper floor. When cider-making commenced, the apples were fed down a chute to the apple-mill, a large circular granite trough. Suspended just above the bottom of the trough was a smaller granite crushing wheel, which was attached to the centre and revolved by hand, the operator walking it round and round the trough until all the apples were pulped. The trough can still be seen at Godolphin, standing in the forecourt as a garden ornament.

A lasting legacy

After the decline of the orchard, the Cider House was used as an agricultural store. During the Schofields' ownership it was put to a new use and turned into a pottery. A small business, The Cider House Pottery, was established by Peter Schofield and Mike Dodd, and ran from there for three years. By the time business ceased, the building was in very poor repair. The north gable end was held up by telegraph poles,

a makeshift measure that prevented the building from collapsing, but when the property was taken over by the National Trust, a more permanent solution was sought.

The Trust secured the building with scaffolding while they raised money for its restoration. A local art teacher, Miss Margery Hall, left a legacy of £100,000 to the Trust to fund a restoration project in Cornwall. Miss Hall's passion was for classical music and she had attended many concerts in Godolphin's King's Room, so her executors decided to dedicate her legacy to the restoration of the Cider House. The walls were cleaned and re-pointed, and the roof timbers were replaced using Douglas fir. It was also given a new slate roof and a bat-chamber was created. Even a lift was installed. After several years of careful planning and three months of even more careful conservation work by local craftsmen and other specialists, it was re-opened in 2015 and is used for exhibitions, education, meetings and other social activities.

Above Telegraph poles supporting the back wall of the Cider House in 2008

Opposite Before and after the restoration

Principles in practice

The Society for the Protection of Ancient Buildings (SPAB) was founded in 1877 by, among others, the designer William Morris and architect Philip Webb, both considered founders of the Arts and Crafts Movement. They saw a need to oppose what they regarded the destructive 'restoration' of old buildings. Morris, in particular, was concerned about attempts to return buildings to an idealised state from their distant past, which often involved the removal of elements added in their more recent history. Instead, he proposed that ancient buildings should be repaired, not restored, so that their entire history would be protected. Sydney Schofield was a member of SPAB, as is his son John, and both earnestly pursued its principles at Godolphin. The same approach is taken today by the National Trust.

Farming today but in a different way

A large part of the Godolphin estate is unsuitable for conventional farming. Evidence of its industrial heritage, whether trace elements in the ground or the warren of mineshafts underneath it, means that the National Trust must balance its priorities for safe public access and sensitive conservation work, just as it does in the house.

The broad cap of Godolphin Hill is covered in wild gorse and bracken, though cattle are allowed onto it throughout the year – weather permitting – to graze and sustain its natural ecology. They keep down intrusive plant species, trampling down the bracken, and help to keep clear the paths that walkers use. The views from the summit are spectacular, extending over Mount's Bay, the southern coast and the Lizard Peninsula.

Reclaimed by nature

The lower part of the land running towards the River Hayle was once the site of intensive mine workings. There the ground has long been stripped of its soil and is dotted with spoil tips and other detritus. Despite this industrial past, the ground is carpeted in heather, which flowers in shades of pink and purple in summer. More importantly, it conceals many of Godolphin's 150 or so mineshafts, and so has been left to overgrow in impenetrable thickets to deter unwary walkers and ramblers.

The area also supports rare bryophyte plants, sometimes known as copper mosses, which thrive on concentrations of metals, which would discourage most other plant growth, and have made the area a Site of Special Scientific Interest. The perimeter walks and the paths around the river are safe and very popular, and rich in plants and wildlife. An environment that was once entirely industrial is now a peaceful and natural space.

Above Making hay on the Godolphin estate

A light organic touch

The estate includes a certain amount of managed woodland, in which a programme of replanting with native species was undertaken by the Trust as soon as it took over the land. The remaining acreage in the arable fields is leased to a local farmer, mainly for grazing and silage-making. A pedigree herd of Red Devon cattle has been established, along with a flock of hardy sheep.

The only crops grown are corn and hay. The grassland is managed on organic principles. Most of the hay is used to feed Godolphin's cattle but if there is a surplus, it is sold to other organic concerns, for example to organic dairy herds kept for the manufacture of organic ice-cream. Several hives of bees are kept on the eastern meadow and Godolphin honey is another popular by-product. Natural unblended honey takes on the flavour of the local wildflowers from which the nectar was gathered and varies from place to place.

The light organic touch of the farming activities has allowed the return of many varieties of flora and fauna, for example the barn owls which nest at the Leeds Shaft, jays and woodpeckers in the trees, and several rare butterflies. Not rare, but conspicuous in a way that is peculiar to Godolphin, is the purple hairstreak. The delight about this butterfly is that it lays its eggs on the buds of oak trees, which are stunted in Godolphin Woods due to the copper and mineral content of the soil. Short trees means we can see the eggs!

To be continued

Visitors enjoy the contrast Godolphin makes with other historic houses. It is neither a fully realised great house complete with formal gardens, nor is it a historic ruin, but something possibly more intriguing than either – an open page of history, an unfinished story.

After completing the essential structural works, the National Trust's focus turned to the renovation of the interior, as can still be seen on open days. Outside the main house, work is going ahead to restore the agricultural buildings, enhance the gardens, continue archaeological investigation and in many other ways.

Godolphin is protected by several regulatory bodies. The house and most of its buildings are listed Grade I or II, as are many architectural details and some artefacts such as the old cider trough in the forecourt. Godolphin is also located in the Cornwall and West Devon Mining Landscape – a UNESCO World Heritage Site dedicated to the counties' mining history – a recognition of its contribution to the advance of industrial development.

All this has brought a new dynamic to Godolphin. With the ongoing programme of discovery and reclamation, the many events held at Godolphin, or simply the pleasure to be found by strolling in its fields and gardens, it is a place that visitors return to again and again. It is no museum dedicated to the past, but very much a hands-on experience.

It has so much to offer: in the estate there is evidence of human occupation going back 3,000 years and remains dated to a time when Godolphin was part of the busiest and richest mining area in the world. The house spans hundreds of years of history, at times owned by those who played key roles on the national stage. Its historical significance cannot be overstated, while its tranquillity today is beautifully understated. It certainly has a long history but also offers exciting future discoveries.

Above **Sunset viewed from Godolphin Hill**